Limited Edition

Design: F. A. Cobb

*Limited to 250 numbered First Edition copies
of which this is number _____.*

Limited Edition

Design: F. A. Cobb

Limited to 250 numbered First Edition copies
of which this is number _____

Beautiful

Arizona

Beautiful Arizona

Text by Paul M. Lewis

First Printing May, 1978
Published by Beautiful America Publishing Company
202 N.W. 21st Avenue, Portland, Oregon 97209
Robert D. Shangle, Publisher

Library of Congress Cataloging in Publication Data

Lewis, Paul M.
  Beautiful Arizona

  1. Arizona—Description and travel—1951-
I. Title
F815.L48   917.0'04'5   78-8732
ISBN 0-915796-40-6
ISBN 0-915796-39-2 pbk.

PHOTO CREDITS

BEAUTIFUL AMERICA PUBLISHING COMPANY

CURRENT BOOKS	FORTHCOMING BOOKS IN 1978	1979 CALENDARS
Utah	Vancouver, B.C.	Texas
Oregon	Massachusetts	Hawaii
Alaska	So. California	Illinois
Hawaii	Pennsylvania	Florida
Arizona	Minnesota	Oregon
Montana	Wisconsin	Colorado
Michigan	Maryland	California
Colorado	Kentucky	New York
Washington	Georgia	Michigan
California	Florida	Washington
No. California	Illinois	Western America
San Francisco	Texas	Beautiful America
British Columbia	Ohio	
California Missions		
Western Impressions		
Lewis & Clark Country		

Send for complete catalog, 50ᶜ

Beautiful America Publishing Company
202 N.W. 21st Avenue
Portland, Oregon 97209

CONTENTS

CREDITS

Lithography by Fremont Litho, Inc., Fremont, California

Color Separations by San Diego Color Service, Inc.
San Diego, California

Book Design by Western Photo Group, Portland, Oregon

INTRODUCTION

The North American continent is as multifaced a piece of business as nature in her obsession for infinite variety ever fashioned. From the brittle arctic latitudes to the subtropical warmth of the southern United States is a land mass with such a variety of personalities that it would seem to reflect nature's extravagant inventiveness to a greater degree than anywhere else on earth.

Within the United States, many individual states, especially in the far western regions of the country, are remarkable for their variety of climate and terrain. California comes quickly to mind, as do the Northwest and Rocky Mountain states. But, somehow, people from other parts of the country don't usually think of the Southwest region as being much more than desert and canyons. Yet, here is one of the states that displays multivaried beauty, rivaling any other area of the country.

Arizona. To start with, it has the world's biggest hole in the ground — the Grand Canyon. Its ponderosa pine forests are the most extensive in the country — lumbering is a very big industry in Arizona, a surprise to folks who thought it was mostly desert washes and canyons (probably from seeing all those Western epics that have been filmed in Arizona). The deserts are there too, mostly in the south and southwest. Up in the northeast, on the mesa lands, gargantuan and grotesquely beautiful towers of rock seem to burst out of the high plateau with the fierce power of elemental forces. These eroded pinnacles stand on a harsh, desert-like landscape, whose beauty is deadly to all but the most tenacious of plant life. Here in Navajo land the vistas are limitless, the colors intense. South of Flagstaff in north-central Arizona is a parcel of earth that partakes of both the monumental and the intimate in landscapery. This is Oak Creek Canyon, surely one of the most beautiful places that was ever invented. Oak Creek has some of the attributes of Grand Canyon — on a smaller scale — softened by dense woods in its northern part.

Mountain and lake environments are the norm in the high country around Flagstaff and in the White Mountains close to the eastern border. Mountain ranges bulge up in every area of the state, but, the volcanic San Francisco Peaks north of Flagstaff, the Whites to the east and the Santa Catalinas and Santa Ritas around Tucson, are some of the highest, with altitudes from about 9,000 to 12,670 feet (Humphreys Peak).

For a touch of topographical whimsy, there is nothing anywhere else quite like the Mogollon Rim that juts up across the east-central part of Arizona like a sheer wall 200 miles long and up to 1,500 feet high along its higher reaches. The Rim delineates two distinct halves of eastern Arizona — the high mesalands to the north and the southern deserts.

With its extreme heat and extreme cold (and all the moderate ranges in between), mountains and deserts, moist and arid climes, and perhaps most important of all, its endless sunshine, you might imagine people would be swarming over the borders of Arizona as if to the Promised Land. And that, as you know, is exactly what has been happening in the second half of the 20th century, courtesy of increased leisure time, super highways, and super automobiles. The city of Phoenix has risen out of the desert like a latter-day version of that legendary bird. The metropolis is a man-created oasis in the midst of a huge agricultural oasis, itself born from the fertile but arid southern Arizona deserts.

The human success at greening up the desert has been both the solution and the problem. Bringing water to Phoenix and the agricultural areas has been a glowing story of achievement in terms of attracting more and more people and growing more and more crops. But Arizona's on-again, off again rivers have about reached their limit (even the Salt, lifeline of Phoenix and the surrounding farmlands, disappears before it can reach west to the Gila; irrigation canals have sucked it dry). More water works, some controversial, are planned to provide for Arizona's still rapidly growing human population. But one begins to wonder if dams and storage reservoirs are the solution *ad infinitum*. The major rivers of interior Arizona like the Salt, the Gila, the Agua Fria, and the Verde, are already harnessed by dams to water Arizona's southern deserts. The demands on the mighty Colorado River are already enormous, both from Arizona and neighboring states. To keep bringing in more water from greater and greater distances to fill the needs of a population that never stops growing seems like an exercise in perpetual motion. There is no end to it.

Many parts of Arizona are so beautiful, in their various ways, that they challenge the capacity of human sensibilities to experience them in all their richness. This is so because man has still not altered them in any way or has been careful to disturb their ecological relationships as little as possible. But as more and more demands are made upon the land — upon the watersheds, the ranges, the grasslands — without letup, it is inevitable that the pure wilderness experience will become harder and harder to find, the sense of being free in a wild, raw nature, will be lost.

One law never changes: to get something, you lose something. Our civilization's progressive mastery of material needs has brought about more and more of an alienation from nature. For most of this century, at least, and until the last few years, we have regarded ourselves as beings somehow apart from nature. But we can't keep on gobbling up the earth's resources without putting ourselves in jeopardy. In the United States, a land extraordinarily endowed with some of the more spectacular natural masterpieces, we are beginning to see the need to limit both our numbers and our activities. Arizona, being perhaps the epitome of all in our country that is beautiful in all the multitude of ways that nature creates beauty, must be one of the first places where we reverse our course, where we *don't* press onward and "improve" every square mile to make it useful. Just by being there, the varied enchantments of Arizona are fulfilling their highest mission. By standing back and admiring them the way they are, we are fulfilling ours.

THE GRANDEST CANYON

"**S**o what's it good for?" the smart-alecky 13-year-old demanded as he looked around at the others, confident he had said something very funny.

He and his parents were standing in a little group of tourists near the Visitor's Center, everyone gazing at the target of the boy's remark. Some of them smiled indulgently at the shrill little weisenheimer. Others obviously wished he'd crawl under one of the larger pieces of rim rock.

For a brief time the gathering had been a silent one. But now the spell was broken. Some people began shifting around restlessly now, anxious to be on their way. Before they had seemed content to just stand and gaze down, down, down into the awful gulf and out over the colossal trench sweeping up and back in tortuous curves from a tiny river a mile below the rim. Now they began shuffling their feet, some of them thinking about getting back to their cars and driving to their motels in town in time to have a good meal and a good night's rest.

After all, they had seen it now. The Grand Canyon of the Colorado River had posed obligingly before their awed gaze, indifferent to their collective and individual "ooohs" and "aaahs."

What is probably the most awesome natural phenomenon in the United States, and quite likely in the whole world, cannot be "done" in a glance from a single viewpoint on the rim. A feature of the earth as vast as the Grand Canyon will always remain, in the literal sense, unknowable. Simple statistics bring this point home very quickly: length, 200 miles; depth, 4,000-6,000 feet; width four to eight miles. But as the early explorers of the canyon discovered, and as the more venturesome visitors still do today, one gets the "feel" of this cosmic cleft in Arizona's Kaibab plateau by putting oneself into it.

Following the lead of the first official exploration in 1869 by John Wesley Powell's expedition, countless numbers have descended into the canyon's mile-deep cavity, on foot or by mule train. There they have become a part of the canyon itself, instead of just passively looking at it from the "outside," so to speak. To get the fullest experience of the canyon, every year hundreds of daredevils do what Powell did. They run the river the full length of its canyon career.

The river. The Colorado River seems so small and still from the rim. How could such an inconsequential ribbon of water have sawed its way through all that rock, no matter how many eons it took? Once down at river level the visitor becomes a believer. The "tiny stream" is a furious, brawling bulldozer, chewing at one bank, then another as it winds its sinuous course through the corridor of rock it has created over 10 million years or so.

(Opposite:) Poppies brighten the stark ramparts of the Superstition Mountains near Phoenix.
(Following Full Page:) The Grand Canyon provides a spectacular background for this tree on Navajo Point.
(Following Page, Above:) The San Francisco Peaks near Flagstaff put on their fall raiment.
(Following Page, Below:) The Yei-bichai Rocks, sacred to primitive desert tribes, are still an awesome presence in Monument Valley.

(Previous Two Pages:) The sparkling waters of Oak Creek spread out in gentle cascades as they course through Oak Creek Canyon near Sedona.

(Opposite:) Chunks of petrified logs lie jumbled like so many candy sticks in a canyon of the Blue Mesa area in Petrified Forest National Park.

(Right:) These magenta cactus blooms furnish some of the desert's most brilliant color.

(Below:) The Verde River provides a setting of desert enchantment northeast of Phoenix.

(Following Two Pages:) Sunset brings deep shadows and brilliant highlights to the South Rim of the Grand Canyon near Mather Point.

(Opposite:) The rim of Sunset Crater glows a dull red just before the entire crater is enveloped in the shadow of the nearby San Francisco Peaks.

(Right:) A balanced rock in the Chiricahua Mountains is unmoved by the forces of nature.

(Below:) Joshua trees and Saguaro cactus share the landscape around Alamo Dam and Reservoir on the Bill Williams River.

(Following Full Page:) Mooney Falls, the tallest of all the Havasu Canyon cataracts, brings green life to the canyon rocks.

(Following Page, Above:) The bleak Superstitions near Phoenix live up to their name as mountains of mystery.

(Following Page, Below:) Autumn applies its colorful paintbrush to the Verde River below Horseshoe Dam.

(Opposite:) Mountain runoff waters the rocks of Wet Canyon, Mt. Graham, near Safford.

(Right:) A fat barrel cactus imparts a red spot of color to the stark desert floor.

(Below:) The orange-red floor of Monument Valley glows under the summer sun.

(Following Full Page:) Wildflowers brighten the slope of O'Leary's Peak in Sunset Crater National Park.

There is more than one way to traverse the canyon. Whether one does it standing up or sitting down, he can't help but begin to feel a bit insignificant down among all that two-billion-year-old rock exposed by the river at the bottom of the inner canyon. Rock that old represents half of the earth's four-billion-year existence. Human beings, on the other hand, have been around for only a million years or so, give or take a few hundred thousand. So it's humble time for us, when we contemplate how infinitesimal a piece of the earth's time scale we occupy.

After we recover from the devastating realization that we're not so much, we can settle down to enjoying the idea that "our" canyon is a special place, a place where a geology lesson covering at least two billion years is presented to us. The top layer of Kaibab and Coconino plateaus were at one or more times in the past covered by a great inland sea.

A lot of people who visit the canyon wonder how it got there. All the ingenious theories about the canyon's creation notwithstanding, the oversimplified facts are, in layman's language, that the plateaus of the canyon region slowly rose while the Colorado River slowly cut into them. The river is still cutting its own narrow trench. Wind and rain and other forces of erosion have accounted for the wide canyon walls at rim level — from four to 18 miles apart. The North Rim plateau (Kaibab) bulges up somewhat higher than the South Rim plateau (Coconino). Consequently, the North Rim is 8,200 feet (at Grand Canyon Village). As an added consequence the ecologies of the two canyon rims are somewhat different. The higher North Rim is cooler and has a thick forest cover. It gets more precipitation, too, with as much as 30 feet of snow during an especially severe winter. The rich, thick Kaibab Forest of the North Rim side is testimony to this. The flora and even the fauna of the two rims are in several instances distinctive, although this distinction is affected by localized climatic variables occuring within the canyon's complicated topography.

Environmental factors, rather than purely physical ones, act as barriers for the canyon's animal inhabitants, as well. Even though the canyon is a monumental gash in the earth, it is not, in this sense, an impassible barrier. Animals can climb down and up steep rock walls. When the living conditions on one level are not suitable for them they will avoid that level. A trip from the river at the bottom of the canyon to the North Rim (5,000 feet) is equivalent to a journey from northern Mexico to northern Canada — several thousand miles.

Over the ages, some animals of the same species have become permanently separated, eventually evolving into lines quite sharply delineated from each other. Two intriguing examples of this are the Kaibab squirrel and the Abert squirrel. Both tassel-eared, these squirrels depend for their livelihood on the ponderosa forests of the canyon. When the ponderosas became separated by the canyon's widening gulf, the two strains of squirrels, once one and the same, became separated from each other and eventually went different ways, evolutionally. The Kaibab, found only in the North Rim ponderosa pine forests, has black underparts and a white tail. The Abert squirrel has large ears, a gray body and tail, with white underparts. It has more living space than its cousin to the north, although it depends for its main diet on the ponderosa pine.

(Previous Page, Above:) Water, cactus, shrubbery, and rock structures combine into a many-textured landscape near Saguaro Lake.
Previous Page, Below:) The Tuzigoot National Monument east of Clarksdale is a prehistoric Indian ruin that was excavated in this century.

One of the most sublime views of the canyon available to human visitors (or to any other animal to whom views are important) is found at Point Sublime, a long promontory that reaches into the chasm from the North Rim. The North Rim is more lavishly endowed with these rocky fingers than the South Rim, doubtless because erosion has cut more deeply into the north side. Drainage patterns and increased precipitation are more formidable erosive forces on the North Rim.

Point Sublime was aptly named by Major Clarence E. Dutton, an army officer who was involved in the surveys of the plateau region in the 1870s, and who described features of the Grand Canyon with an eloquence that has never been surpassed. Standing on a narrow neck of land almost 7,500 feet high, one is thrust into the yawning abyss and sometimes enveloped in the blue and purple haze that fills the vast spaces around and under him. The prickly thrill that comes in such a situation reminds me of times I have been in a train going over a high bridge whose supporting structures are invisible from inside the passenger coach. The sensation of resting on nonexistent supports produces the same kind of pleasurable anxiety, it seems to me, as that which one experiences as he stands on this peninsula of rock and surveys the near and far scene in the stupendous kaleidoscope of light and land that stretches away from him to all points of the compass.

The view from Point Sublime is studded with the buttes and temples that hug the North Rim, backgrounded by the colossal side canyons gouged into the Redwall limestone like oversize band concert shells. These amphitheaters are everywhere, in the near view and the far view, on both sides of the canyon. The South Rim, about six miles across the gulf, is 1,000 feet below. In the endless play of light, the South Rim seems to move nearer or farther away, depending on whether it is in brilliant sunlight or in shadow. The reds and the marble-grays of the walls are somber and bright in turn.

For 150 miles, east to the west, the panorama of the canyon and of northern Arizona beyond is displayed before the observer on Point Sublime. The tireless Colorado is visible on both sides of the viewpoint, and the deep, dark inner canyon appears much closer here than at any other spot on the North Rim. (On the South Rim, where erosion has not carried the canyon walls as far back, the inner canyon is more accessible visually). The South Rim's Havasupai Point pushes its huge mass into the canyon to the west, adding its immensity to the bewildering variety of basins, buttes, walls, ridges, and promontories that seem to make chaotic nonsense out of the Grand Canyon. The canyon's basically coherent structure also becomes visible on Point Sublime, as it does on no other Grand Canyon overlook, because of the *amount* of canyon that can be seen from here. The horizontal layers of rock are everywhere the same, with only an occasional fault line or fold. From the topmost layer of light-colored Coconino sandstone to the very bottom of the inner canyon where the river is still slowly slicing into the terribly hard, two-billion-year-old schist and gneiss, half of the entire life history of the earth is revealed.

Point Sublime has one serious drawback, from the point of view of the auto tourist. The road to it is not paved, nor is it well maintained. It has ruts and a high center in some places, forcing cars to slow down. But then, anyone who comes to Point Sublime with the notion of getting there and out in a hurry is missing the point of Point Sublime. The visitor, who hopes to acquire some understanding of a natural phenomenon that represents a time scale inconceivably more vast than human experience can encompass, must meet this wilderness on its own terms and leave behind the pervasive obsession with schedules that rules our technological age.

27

Easier access are Bright Angel Point and Cape Royal, both east of Point Sublime and served by paved roads. Grand Canyon Lodge on Bright Angel Point is perched right on the edge of Bright Angel Canyon and affords guests of the lodge an intimate glimpse of the deep chasm, its sub-canyons, and its formations. Cape Royal has several major viewpoints, including Point Imperial, highest of any rim location at 8,801 feet. Point Imperial, like the other North Rim vantage points, looks down on the South Rim and the immense plateau beyond. Here, in the easterly bend of the canyon, the view takes in the Painted Desert and Echo Cliffs to the east. Far to the northeast (90 miles) Navajo Mountain can be seen with the Vermillion Cliffs to the west.

The South Rim of the canyon is the more "civilized," being closer to population centers of Arizona and consequently easier to get to. Visitor accommodations in Grand Canyon National Park are concentrated on the South Rim because that is where most tourists congregate. But we have been visiting points on the North Rim, and, before we can talk about the South Rim, we have to get there. How is that accomplished? The distance from rim to rim in this part of the canyon is only about 12 miles. The automobiles being turned out these days are not very good at leaping over a mile-deep chasm 12 miles wide. So, unless we decide to abandon our cars on the North Rim and cross the canyon via the Kaibab Trail suspension footbridge, we have to go the long way around — 217 miles to be exact — to get to the South Rim. It's a marvelous drive and worth every one of those 217 miles.

(The footbridge — serving canyon hikers, mules, and assorted canyon wildlife — is the only canyon crossing. Consequently, the Kaibab trail, starting at Grand Canyon Lodge on the North Rim, is the only cross-canyon trail, 20.6 miles from rim to rim.)

From the thick Kaibab National Forest of the North Rim, State Highway 67 takes us down from the plateau into House Rock Valley, a wild buffalo range. The buffalo are rarely seen from the highway, however. The road heads straight north and then east and north along the colorful Vermillion Cliffs. Then we come to Marble Canyon and Navajo Bridge — the only span across the Colorado in the 1,000-mile distance between Moab, Utah, and Lake Mead.

Before we get to the bridge we may decide to follow a dirt road that takes off from the highway and leads north along the Colorado River to Lee's Ferry. The site has associations with some of this country's more violent chapters of history. The ferry was operated in the 1870s by John D. Lee, a former Mormon leader. The enterprise was ended when Lee was executed in 1877 by United States forces in connection with the massacre 20 years before of a group of settlers coming in from Arkansas and Mississippi.

Back on the main highway we cross the bridge, stop on the other side and take a good look at Marble Canyon, where the Grand Canyon of the Colorado begins with a miniature version of the bigger one farther west. The road now turns due south and links up with U. S. 89. We drive along the Echo Cliffs, on our left, and of course cannot resist a shout to test whether the cliffs are properly named. A return shout gives us our answer.

After some 20 miles we come to Cedar Ridge and The Gap, Indian trading posts, for we are now passing through the western part of the huge Navajo Indian Reservation. If it's the warm time of year we may see Navajo shepherds along the way, tending their flocks in the arroyos. The Navajo hogans can be seen here, too. Now we're into the western edge of the Painted Desert and approaching the Little Colorado River gorge. Just below Cameron, on the Little Colorado, we turn due west on State 64, heading for the South Rim. On the way we have some soul-satisfying views of the gorge, but the ultimate in viewpoints is reached at Desert View, about 32 miles along this road, and on the eastern edge of the South Rim. Desert View is so named because it is such a marvelous visual vantage point for seeing the Painted Desert, spreading out on the eastern landscape in all of its rich colors. That is only the beginning of what Desert View can offer. From here there is a variety of scenery surpassing that of any other point on either rim of the canyon, including a long westerly view that takes in not only the ribbon of the Colorado far below but more of the inner canyon itself. At Desert View the South Rim has been eroded back farther than at other points on this rim, and the canyon is therefore more open.

West of Desert View on the South Rim are many other magnificent viewpoints before the east rim drive reaches the Visitor Center and Grand Canyon Village. Lipan, Moran, Grandview, Yaki, and Yavapai points all have their distinctive canyon outlooks. This portion of the rim is the most visited area of Grand Canyon. If one comes for solitary contemplation he should have stayed on the other side. The rim drive follows west some distance past Grand Canyon Village — a rather "citified" agglomeration of buildings and a campground installed to serve the flood of tourists.

On this short spur there are several more points where certain canyon features are highlighted. Trail View, the first of these, is a good place to watch hikers and mule parties of canyon explorers on the one-mule-wide, cross-canyon Kaibab Trail which heads up at Yaki Point, a short distance to the east. Way down (3,200 feet) below the rim is a wide, flat shelf called the Tonto Plateau, with a green oasis named Indian Gardens. Trail parties usually stop here for a rest before continuing the descent or climb of the steep south wall. Across the canyon is a steep side chasm in which flows Bright Angel Creek, a flashing little stream paralleled by the Kaibab Trail on its way to the North Rim.

Maricopa and Hopi points are next, offering wide-angle views of vast canyon stretches. Many of the bewildering varieties of rock structures within the canyon have names and can be identified by anyone with a detailed map and an interest in this sort of activity. Sunsets are a specialty of Hopi Point. The wide view of the canyon is especially stunning in the orange-red light of the setting sun, and a little later, with the sun already over the horizon, the river reflects the pastel colors of the evening sky.

Mohave Point is close by the the west and therefore the long view from it is not much changed from the two previous points, but Mohave is well situated to allow a close inspection of the steep walls of nearby points on the South Rim. The most coherent layer in the canyon walls is the Redwall limestone which occurs about halfway down and is up to 400 feet thick. Iron oxides that wash down from overlying strata contribute its brilliant red color, except on points or pinnacles where nothing overlies it; then the color is a blueish-gray. The road comes to an end a bit beyond Pima Point, at Hermit's Rest. The point juts far out into the canyon, so that distance views are very good indeed. Havasupai Point bulks large about eight miles west, and Point Sublime

is about the same distance across the canyon on the North Rim. The volcanic cones of Mt. Trumbull and Mt. Logan, 60 miles westward, can be seen on clear days. Monument Rapids, one of Colorado's most formidable, is visible from this perch, and sometimes, the noise of the rapids' violent wave action can be heard. On the North Rim plateau west of Pima Point can be seen a great fault or fracture line, where the rock layers broke vertically during the general uplift of the whole land mass. The line is notched in a V shape by erosive forces acting upon this weak section.

Westward beyond this overlook there are a great many stupendous sights to be seen from the rim, but, they require somewhat more individual effort from the visitor, since the road ends at Hermit's Rest, just beyond Pima Point. There are many ways to see the canyon, including those portions other than the ones in the limited areas of the canyon that are accessible by road. The famous mule trains that carry tourists down to the river are a marvelous means of participating in the sense of adventure the canyon offers. For both mule riders and trail hikers there is even a place to stay overnight in Bright Angel Canyon. Phantom Ranch, near Bright Angel Creek, is a delightful oasis that fits unobtrusively into the canyon bottom as if it were part of the canyon architect's original plan.

One of the really adventurous ways to "do" Grand Canyon is by boat, and every year hundreds of free spirits go barreling down the Colorado in parties guided by experienced river runners. They may travel a short stretch or go all the way to Lake Mead and the canyon's end. This way they get an entirely new "feel" of the giant chasm not possible from the rim. Marble Gorge, near Lee's Ferry, offers the inner canyon visitor a "candy-striped" lower wall of Redwall limestone that resembles marbling. Nankoweap Canyon, on the North Rim near Point Imperial, is a popular stopping place for river parties. A rugged 12-mile trail from the river connects with Saddle Mountain and rewards the physically fit who try it with views of some of the most awesome scenery in the Whole Grand Canyon. Here is the Kwagunt Rapid, where the Colorado roars with authority, and just below, the juncture of the Little Colorado with the big river. The waters of the two rivers are in stark contrast, the clear turquoise of tributary stream blending with the muddy flow of the main channel. Farther along, the cliffs of the Cape Royal area push up as high as 8,000 feet.

The visitor who would have pretensions of getting to know the Grand Canyon of the Colorado should have several months to spend at the task and be able to hike some of the trails in addition to roaming the rims and riding the river. In particular, the trails of the more remote western section of the canyon lead into spots of lush beauty that would seem hardly possible to one accustomed to the impression of stark grandeur that a rim or air view of the canyon gives. One of the most satisfying wilderness experiences available in Grand Canyon National Park can be had by hiking the Thunder River trail which heads just outside of the park boundaries on the North Rim, 18 miles southwest of Big Springs Ranger Station. The trail drops down by steps through the Kaibab National Forest in a generally southeasterly direction to Thunder River about 15 miles west of Point Sublime. Thunder River lives up to its name, most particularly at Thunder Spring, which roars with soul-satisfying intensity as it plunges a half-mile down a steep ravine into Tapeats Creek. The creek courses three more precipitous miles (dropping 500 feet) to the Colorado. The trail runs out at Tapeats Creek but the intrepid hiker can follow the creek to his destination.

(Previous Two Pages:) The Giant's Thumb is one of the powerful rock structures that dominate in Oak Creek Canyon.

The Grand Canyon was home to human beings long before the white man discovered it. Remains of Indian dwellings and artifacts on the North Rim and along some of the lower canyon walls attest to this. Now, discounting the tourist service areas on the South and North Rims — the canyon shelters no permanent inhabitants, with the exception of one remarkable instance. This is in Havasu Canyon, a lush green paradise that seems to sum up all that is possible in the way of natural beauty. Here in this remote corner of Grand Canyon, about 35 miles west of Grand Canyon Village, live the Havasupai Indians. The Havasupais have inhabited their little canyon for hundreds of years. Nobody knows just how many hundreds, but they have obviously found the good life in their protected niche. They have pleasant summers and mild winters, and an abundant supply of fresh water. They grow most of their own food during a long season, and their isolated canyon situation that formerly protected them from marauding tribes, now protects them from many of the pernicious influences of the 20th century. Because they are within the sheltering borders of Grand Canyon National Park, it will be a long time before any alien lifestyle encroaches upon their simple, relatively carefree existence.

How does one get to see this Shangri-la? Not by car. There are no roads into Havasu Canyon. The only way is to hike or ride (horseback) from Hualapai Hilltop on the South Rim. It's eight miles to the village of Supai in the canyon. The Havasupai Tribal Council has control of access to their canyon, but visitors are welcomed and may partake of food and accommodations in their village. The canyon, actually, is less than half a mile wide and 2½ miles long. Its permanent and reliable water supply comes from Havasu Creek, which steps down into the canyon over three gorgeous waterfalls — Navajo, Havasu, and Mooney. The creek's water is a dazzling turquoise-blue created from the reflection of fine clay particles in the stream. The creek flows from pool to pool in its cool, forested glens, attracting many birds. Cormorants, grebes, and teals are seen here, as are the bottom-walking water ouzels, hummingbirds, and, of course, woodpeckers and kingbirds.

Unfortunately, the pressure of visitors is beginning to have some adverse effects on this sheltered haven in the desert. Steep canyon walls cannot keep out tourist hordes once word gets around that one of the world's beauty spots is waiting to be discovered. The delicate charms of Havasu Canyon cannot long withstand the pressure of numbers. Perhaps the Havasupais will be wise enough to restrict entry to their Shangri-la before its beauty is defiled and its magic destroyed.

NOT SO GRAND, BUT JUST AS GORGEOUS

Flagstaff and Prescott in north-central Arizona preside over a region of truly astounding natural beauty, manifested in a variety of topographic features. Mountains and valleys, forest and desert, canyons, rivers, and lakes are strewn over the land in such close conjunction that one is tempted to see it all as a kind of scenic model set up by the Celestial Architect to inspire His settings for other parts of the world.

Immediately north of Flagstaff are the San Francisco Mountains, Arizona's highest. On the south, between Flagstaff and Sedona, is the fabulous and famous Oak Creek Canyon. West of it, Sycamore Canyon, in the midst of a large primitive area, stretches 17 miles to White Horse Lake on the north. This is ponderosa pine country, in a part of the Kaibab National Forest, which also takes in large areas on the North and South Rims of the Grand Canyon. Canyon visitors find Flagstaff and the town of Williams, 31 miles west, good places from which to launch trips to the big Colorado River ditch up north. From picturesque Williams it's a straight shot about 58 miles to the South Rim.

Some of the bonuses that the Scenic Sculptor threw in when He made Arizona are the marvelous perspectives that are available from one beauty spot to the next. This is abundantly evident north and east of Flagstaff. That city is already on high ground (6,900 feet altitude), and just on its doorstep is some higher ground — the San Francisco Peaks. From the summit of these mountains you can see forever, especially from Mt. Humphreys' lofty 12,260-foot crown. The panoramic view takes in the Grand Canyon itself, on the north; Oak Creek Canyon to the south; and, on the near and far eastern horizons, Sunset Crater's dormant volcanic cone and the Painted Desert.

North of Sunset Crater is Wupatki National Monument, which contains hundreds of ruins of Indian villages. And just south of Flagstaff is Walnut Canyon National Monument, where the remains of 800-year-old Indian cliff dwellings are preserved in the horseshoe-shaped canyon.

Wupatki is situated in the high northern desert that surrounds the Grand Canyon country, so it is rather a novelty to find a big river nearby — the Little Colorado River. More surprising still is to discover Grand Falls — of Niagara proportions — on this river. This cataract is 185 feet high and spills down over a broad front, when the river is high enough. The falls' flow is determined by the runoff from the Mogollon Rim to the south, greatest during the spring snow melt.

(Previous Full Page:) The harsh aspect of the Wupatki National Monument seems to belie the fact that the area was once farmed by pueblo Indians.
(Previous Page, Above:) Lavender sand verbena carpet the desert near Yuma.
(Previous Page, Below:) Winter brushes Oak Creek Canyon with a cottony blanket of snow.

This area is especially thrilling to tour in the springtime. Then U.S. 180 (the scenic route to the Grand Canyon) becomes a road through a garden of alpine wildflowers splashing their bright colors against the red-rock earth, under a deep blue sky sometimes dotted with billowing thunderheads.

A little farther from Flagstaff, but this time in a southeasterly direction, is one of those curiosities that sets the mind to speculating on the nature of things and the state of the universe. Meteor Crater is a very impressive hole in the ground just south of Interstate 40. It measures a mile across, three miles around, and is 570 feet deep. According to the people who are good at figuring out such things, it was caused by a 60,000-ton meteor about 50,000 years ago.

This high country is a part of the Coconino plateau, itself a part of the general Kaibab bulge that swells to its highest point on the North Rim of the Grand Canyon (9,300 feet). But, the upwelling is so gradual it is barely discernible. The name, *Kaibab* — "mountain lying down" — is quite appropriate.

One of the true masterpieces of canyon-cutting has been accomplished by Oak Creek, after a big fault in the Coconino sandstone started things going. The famous canyon has been photographed about as much as *Numero Uno* to the north and is described by some commentators as the single most beautiful place in North America. One reason for its special luster is the variety of plant life within the canyon. Oak Creek contains many kinds of environments, and, as a result, many kinds of plants. A visitor can discover this for himself, starting from the lower canyon at Sedona, where the giant red rock canyon walls and structures startle the visual sense and furnish a painterly backdrop for the pretty little town. Among the well-known buttes here are Bell Rock and Cathedral Rock.

Upper Oak Creek Canyon narrows as it rises toward 7,000 feet. The plant life changes from the desert vegetation of the lower canyon to that found in cooler, more northern latitudes. Fir species predominate on the cooler slopes, ponderosa pine on the warmer. Maple, sycamore, oak, and aspen are represented in thick stands on the canyon floor; their seasonal color changes provide a surfeit of bedazzlement to the eye in this already multicolored canyon.

Human beings are not the only ones who appreciate Oak Creek Canyon. Some of the other canyon residents are deer and mountain lion, and, on the upper levels, wild turkey. Here, too, as in all of the country's canyonlands, the little canyon wren's operatic tones are heard.

(Previous Full Page:) Toroweap Point on the North Rim is a good place to get two long views of the Grand Canyon, one horizontal and one straight down.

(Previous Page, Above:) Saguaro cactus in Tucson Mountain Park point black fingers at the fiery glow of the sunset sky.

(Previous Page, Below:) Oak Creek Canyon's Cathedral Rocks seem quite improbable as seen from the perspective of a Sedona apple orchard.

(Opposite:) The Mogollon Rim country possesses some of Arizona's loveliest landscapes.

(Right:) An organ pipe cactus enriches some of Arizona's surrealistic scenery.

(Below:) The Vermillion Cliffs line the route of travelers through House Rock Valley in northern Arizona.

(Previous Two Pages:) The Watchtower at Desert View on the South Rim of the Grand Canyon watches over the Colorado River snaking through an intricate maze of gorges.

(Opposite:) "The Island" rises from the depths of Walnut Canyon, with its ruins of cliff dwellings tucked into the ledges.

(Right:) The prickly pear cactus does its best to light up the desert with yellow flowers.

(Below:) The snow-draped Four Peaks Mountains near Phoenix lend a wintry background over prickly pear cactus on the desert floor.

(Following Two Pages:) Spider Rock points its long, slender spire skyward from the floor of Canyon de Chelly National Monument.

(Previous Full Page:) The overhanging wall of Canyon de Chelly overpowers the White House Ruins near the base of the mammoth rock structure.

(Previous Page, Above:) The eastern end of Grand Canyon begins at Lees Ferry, seen here with the canyon walls reflected in the waters of the Colorado River.

(Previous Page, Below:) The Hualapai Mountains as seen from Kingman at the end of the day.

(Opposite:) Late afternoon brings a warming glow to Lipan Point in the Grand Canyon.

(Right:) A close look at the barrel cactus in bloom.

(Below:) Rudbekias growing on a little island in the East Fork of the Black River.

THE VERDE VALLEY

Stretching to the southeast between Prescott and Sedona is a rocky valley of great beauty and wild character. The Verde River begins its career in north-central Yavapai County and flows through a remote basin cut into the Coconino Plateau. The river and the valley are nourished by waters that seep into them from the plateau above. One of the gorgeous results of this arrangement occurs at Montezuma Well, a cup-shaped lake deep below the surrounding terrain, 1,750 feet in diameter and 65 feet deep. Many kinds of wildlife are drawn to this place, including more than a hundred butterfly species. A few miles southwest of the lake is Montezuma Castle National Monument, perched on a cliff. Built by an ancient Indian tribe, it is a place of mystery today. The middle part of the valley is rolling range about 20 miles wide. Its lower reaches are bounded by the varicolored walls of the Mogollon Rim on the northeast and the Mazatzal Mountains to the south.

The valley is strewn with abandoned mining towns, some of them making a comeback. The most celebrated of the latter is Jerome, a former ghost town that has pulled itself together and is thriving on the tourist trade. In its "fat cat" days Jerome was one of the richest mining communities in the West, with a population of 15,000. After the mines closed down in the early 1950s, the head count dropped to 200. Its new-found success as a tourist town is owing largely to the charm of its setting on the shoulders of the Black Hills (Mingus Mountain) a mile above sea level.

Just as Jerome relates to the past, Arcosanti, about 30 miles due south, is a community of the future. Arcosanti, the dream and creation of architect Paolo Soleri, is located in a steep canyon overlooking the Agua Fria River. A city to house up to 3,500 people is being built on about nine acres of an 860-acre tract. The main building will rise 20 stories from the top of the canyon and other structures will be built into the canyon wall.

(Previous Full Page:) San Xavier Mission near Tucson gleams like pure alabaster in the late day Arizona sun.

(Previous Page, Above:) The Painted Desert in northern Arizona basks undisturbed in the warm sun.

(Previous Page, Below:) Springtime weaves a lavish carpet of color near Wickenburg.

(Previous Full Page:) The San Francisco Peaks near Flagstaff get a good helping of winter snow.

(Previous Page, Above:) The Plomosa Mountains, near Quartzsite, receive the last rays of the day's sun.

(Previous Page, Below:) Beautiful Canyon Lake is a scenic jewel among the varied desert landscapes along the Apache Trail east of Phoenix.

DESERTS — HIGH, LOW AND HOT

One obvious physical fact is the presence of high-country deserts and lowland deserts. The great Kaibab upwarp carries the mesas and plateaus of the northern half to altitudes that reach their highest point on the North Rim of the Grand Canyon (9,300 feet). The southern deserts, beginning south of the Mogollon Rim and stretching southward into Mexico, are lower and hotter, but relieved by mountain oases, particularly in the southeastern sector.

The presence of Phoenix gives the south-central desert more notoriety than the other arid areas. The establishment of such a huge city in the midst of seemingly inhospitable terrain is, of course, dependent on lifelines and ingenuity. The lifelines are the Salt, Verde, and Gila rivers which come together in this area. The ingenuity is represented by the man-made lakes to the north and east that hold water in storage from these rivers, not only providing water for Phoenix but also making possible the existence of a rich agricultural economy in the areas around the city.

Arizona's big city is unusual, not only for where it is but for what it is — a very fine place to live, as more and more people are finding out. Phoenix and the resort towns around it are growing at an explosive rate, filling with refugees from cold winters and humid summers in other parts of the country. Nobody needs the Chamber of Commerce to tell them that the climate is very dry and very healthy, as these facts are well known. And while summer's heat is fierce, Arizonans have developed the necessity of living with it into a high art form. Homes, for instance, are built and oriented so that maximum benefit is derived from air conditioning.

But besides air conditioning, Phoenix has the advantage of being a well-planned city. Many parks are located in and around it, including South Mountain Park, the biggest city park in the world. Much of the parkland around Phoenix has been left in its original wilderness state. And world-famous Scottsdale is just east of the main city. Scottsdale was carefully planned to be "the most western town in the West." Its stylish good taste reflects both the money that went into its conception and the money that has gravitated to it as a sort of spa for the well-to-do.

North of Phoenix the desert begins a gradual rise that continues to the rim country in the state's middle. The cactus and other desert flora yield to juniper and pine near and on the rim, while spectacular arroyos slash into the land. There are a number of ghost towns between Phoenix and Prescott, and some of them are making a try at reincarnation, or at least reinvigoration. Wickenburg, 55 miles northwest of Phoenix, is no ghost town, but it does retain a lot of the Old West trappings, such as hitching posts and false fronts.

The superhighway that connects Phoenix and Flagstaff also goes through some interesting country. Just 20 miles north is Pioneer Arizona, a re-creation of Southwest history in the manner of Williamsburg. The Agua Fria Canyon east of the highway and north of New River is easily accessible for an impromptu hike or for more serious backpacking trips.

THE HIGH MOUNTAINS

The White Mountains of the east and the San Francisco Peaks of north central Arizona are the kings of Arizona's high country. In this age when winter sports are engaged in more than ever before, both areas have become centers of skiing and related activities. But their prime mission, as far as Arizonans are concerned, is to rise above Arizona's hot summer. They are real cool mountains in the real sense, a vacationland that is an alternative to the hot, dry desert country.

The Whites are really a continuation of the Mogollon plateau, carrying that highland up to 11,590 feet at Mt. Baldy, where three major rivers begin their careers — the Little Colorado, the White, and the Black. This is Apache country, being on the Fort Apache Indian Reservation. This reservation and the San Carlos reservation just south of it occupy a large chunk of east-central Arizona. Both Apache tribes are going in heavily for recreational development of their mountains, lakes, and streams, to supplement the livelihood they wrest from their vast grazing lands and farmlands. There is even a miniature version of the Grand Canyon here — the Salt River Canyon, which forms part of the border between the two reservations.

Arizona has a big lumber industry. A large share of those wood products come from the White Mountain forests of Douglas fir and ponderosa pine.

The famed Coronado Trail (now U. S. 666) runs through the White and the Blue mountains on its route between Springerville and Clifton. In so doing it becomes another one of those patented scenic mountain highway spectaculars. Besides the spectacular forest scenery, especially in the fall when brilliant aspens highlight the woodlands, there are long vistas of the terrain to the west, specifically the Mogollon Rim country. The route's southern segment passes the Clifton-Morenci Mining District, where an enormous open-pit copper mine is located.

(Previous Page, Above:) Ocotillo and Teddy bear cactus dot the desert in the Trigo Mountains area.
(Previous Page, Below:) Palo Verde in full bloom near Cave Creek provides a soft-line contrast to other desert vegetation.
(Previous Full Page:) Mountains, desert, and cactus typify much of the terrain around Phoenix. This scene is in the Saguaro Lake area.

NORTH TO NAVAJOLAND

The almost unearthly, stark grandeur of the Four Corners country is well represented in Arizona's piece of it. Erosive forces have had their way to such an extent, that much of this high mesa land is carved up into monumental forms whose beauty is so far from the gentle, pastoral kind we ordinarily associate with natural scenes, that the mind is numbed at first by the visual impact.

This is the domain of the Navajos, whose reservation lands cover more than 25,000 square miles of the Four Corners area, the most extensive Indian reservation in the country. Enclosed within this vast area is the Hopi Reservation. The two tribes have been among the most successful of the Indian peoples in maintaining their traditions and identities in the midst of the industrial world.

One of the beautiful rock fortress hideouts carved into the plateau by wind and water is the Canyon de Chelly. Here the Navajos of the past found refuge from their enemies. Here today's Navajos preserve their way of life within the 1,000-foot sheltering walls of the canyon. There are two major canyons: de Chelly and del Muerto. The latter is more confined and gentler, being a tributary canyon. The red-orange walls are not just sheer; sometimes they are overhanging, and in these sites one is more likely to find the ancient ruins of the Anasazi, the cliff-dwellers. Such a relic is White House Ruin. Others are Mummy Cave and Antelope House ruins.

One of the purely natural masterpieces of the canyon is Spider Rock, whose double spires rise 800 feet out of the canyon floor. Spider Woman, a Navajo deity, inhabits this great knife-blade of rock. She may still be at work weaving some of her colorful cloth, for her dwelling catches and refracts the many different colorations and nuances of sunlight as the day moves from dawn to dusk.

Monument Valley, on the Arizona-Utah border, is really one of Mother Nature's best efforts in regard to red-rock sculpture. The cliffs, pinnacles, buttes, and monoliths are not just gigantic. They are shaped and sculptured as if by a hand applying a conscious art to the task; the fact that they are the accidental creations of a mindless erosive force is hard to accept. Everywhere one looks the monuments are there in their varied forms, and the effect is magical and mesmerizing. This is a Navajo Tribal Park, and the Navajos have clothed these rock structures in their rich mythology.

In the southwestern part of Navajoland flows a stretch of the Little Colorado. Along the river and stretching to the east lie the Badlands called the Painted Desert. The colors of the rock layers are rich and diverse, occuring in bands of stratified rock that contain various combinations of manganese and iron oxides. This remarkable swath of rocky desert extends nearly 200 miles from the Petrified Forest area to the Grand Canyon. Petrified Forest National Park, just off U. S. 40 near Holbrook, contains the largest amount of petrified wood anywhere. There are whole logs as well as cross-sections of colorful mineralized trees.

Near the western border of Navajoland, the Little Colorado River puts on a show of its own just before it gives up its identity and joins the big Colorado. The Little Colorado River Gorge, some 30 miles west of Cameron, is a masterpiece of its kind. It doesn't have the depth of Big Brother next door but is much narrower, which makes it seem deeper.

THE MOGOLLON RIM

The western part of this 200-mile-long escarpment begins in the geographical center of the state, near the southern end of the Verde Valley, and spreads east, effectively cutting Arizona's eastern half in two. The south-facing Rim cuts off the southern desert country from the forest and lake terrain that it carries on its back. The Mogollon cliffs rise to 1,500 feet in some places. On this odd uplifted area sea fossils can be found, showing that the Rim country was once an ancient ocean bed, elevated 7,000 feet above the sea level of today.

Tonto Natural Bridge, near Payson at the Rim's western end, is the largest natural arch in the world, lifting 185 feet above the bed of a stream. It is composed of white limestone and red coral, and under it are the ruins of former Indian dwellings.

A rim road follows the contour of the escarpment, with what is, naturally, an unbeatable view. But it is not open year-round. The main stretch of the pine-covered Rim is also followed closely by State 260, which climbs up onto the escarpment shortly after Payson. This gives travelers a fine, close view of the Rim's sandstone rock layers. The high ride along the Rim also affords a wide vista of the Tonto Basin, as the heart of the Rim country is called. The drive is the scenic equal of some other incredible views with which Arizona is gifted. In the deep pine woods below the western wall, between State 87 and Kohl's Ranch, an unimproved road runs close to the towering cliffs, with glimpses of their imposing sides through the trees.

The Mogollon Rim country is a paradise for wild game, with its many trout streams and lakes. The forests are home to black bear, deer, and elk, in addition to smaller animals. Some of the lakes, like Bear Canyon, Woods Canyon, and Willow Spring, are near the edge of the Rim and easily accessible from the rim road.

(Previous Two Pages:) Rock formations on the bluff at Red Rock Crossing dominate this Oak Creek landscape.

The West and Southwest

"Summer is a-comin' in" has a special meaning around Yuma and the low southwestern deserts. The summers are not only sizzling hot, but terribly dry, weather that is reinforced by the sea-level elevations. The desert holds sway here, and there really would not be much else, except for the presence of the Colorado and Gila rivers. One can see mountains on the horizons, but they represent a distinctly minority viewpoint.

Winter is a good enough time for visiting this desert country, but autumn and spring are the best. As spring blends into summer, the winds rise, and sometimes so do sandstorms. A large extent of desert around Yuma has been made fertile by water from the dams on the Colorado. Here is, in fact, one of the largest areas of artificial irrigation in Arizona. Vast orchards and fields encircle the city. Citrus fruits, dates, and peaches are grown, as are cotton, alfalfa, wheat, and barley.

The desert is really full of life, some of which flourishes in what would be impossibly harsh conditions for other life forms. The town of Gila Bend, 120 miles east of Yuma in the middle of some of the more fascinating desert and mountain terrain, is an appropriate headquarters from which desert-watchers can make forays into the area. Desert though it is, it is far from unrelieved barren wastes. The Gila River green belt, between Yuma and Gila Bend, brings in a great number of migratory birds and provides habitat for other forms of wildlife.

South of this belt and on into Mexico the mesquite and yucca are everywhere, growing to giant size, but the real king of the desert is the creosote bush. On the Mexican border, 60 miles south of Gila Bend, Organ Pipe National Monument is a preserve where many different forms of cactus flourish. Hundreds of bird species are attracted to this area as well, for the cacti bloom at various times, providing enticement from March through June. The monument's namesake cactus, the organ pipe, is so-called because its branches resemble the pipes of an organ, growing almost straight up from the base of the main trunk. Like the other giant cactus, the saguaro, it blooms in late May or early June. Smaller species bloom earlier: the hedgehog cactus displays its brilliant rose-purple cups in March; the whip-like ocotillo unfolds a big fiery-red flower in April; the palo verde glows yellow in early May.

Nearer to Gila Bend, on the west, is Painted Rocks State Historic Park. Here is an outstanding collection of Indian rock paintings and writings dating from prehistoric times.

Much of the territory north of Yuma along the Colorado River is in reservation land and wildlife preserves. The Trigo and Chocolate Mountain ranges west of the road to Parker include the big Imperial National Wildlife Refuge, part of which is in California. East of the highway is the Kofa Game Range, in the rugged Kofa Mountains, the home of mountain lions, desert bighorn sheep, coyote, and kit fox. The Kofas are a sanctuary for many birds, too, of which the gambel quail and mourning doves are most often seen. Palm Canyon, in an exceptionally rugged part of the Kofas, shelters the only palm tree stand in Arizona.

Between Organ Pipe National Monument and Tucson is the huge Papago Indian Reservation of three million acres. Visitors may attend some of the traditional feasts and festivities of the Papagos such as the All-Indian Rodeo and Fair in Sells.

SOUTH AND EAST

One would expect the desert to be omnipresent in Arizona's southern reaches, but east and south of Phoenix are a variety of environments where the desert is modified and even replaced by mountains and forest. Directly east of Phoenix, and not very far away, are the fabled Superstition Mountains, where the legend of the Lost Dutchman mine keeps would-be prospectors roaming through the rugged mountain ramparts for a treasure that may exist only in their minds. The more easily accessible parts of these mountains unfortunately show the signs of being near a great metropolitan center. Refuse litters the trails. But in the more remote parts of these very rugged lava mountains, signs of human intrusion are not to be found. Modern human intrusion, that is. The Indians have, at one time or another, decorated the rocks of Hieroglyphic Canyon in the Superstitions with petroglyphs.

Phoenix to Globe (88 miles) is a trip that offers the maximum in scenery via either a southern leg (U. S. 60) through the mountain wilderness or the northerly Apache Trail (State 88) which touches three big Salt River lakes) — Canyon, Apache, and Roosevelt — just north of the Superstitions. Four Peaks, just north of Apache Lake, affords a marvelous view of the Salt River Valley to the southwest and Tonto Basin under the Mogollon Rim to the northeast. The Four Peaks area is at the southern end of the Mazatzal range and can be reached via a forest road.

Tucson, 116 miles from Phoenix in the southeast corner, is the Valhalla of wintertime sun worshippers. It's right in the desert but surrounded by mountain chains, and some of the best of both environments is in the Tucson vicinity. The city's 2,400-foot elevation helps give it year-round liveability. The Santa Catalina Mountains north of town and the Santa Ritas to the south are the tallest and most extensive of the six separate mountain systems in the area. All of this land around Tucson, the desert and the mountains, is preserved for the public. For example, Saguaro National Monument (two sections — east and west of town) provides protected growing space for the spectacular giant Saguaro cactus, of which the monument has a great number. Tucson Mountain Park, also on the west side, is a large preserve containing both high desert and mountain areas, including the famed Arizona-Sonora Desert Museum. Hiking trails to the high vantage points command sweeping views of the Avra Valley on the west.

The Desert Museum is a carefully arranged "living" exhibit of the plants and animals found in the Sonora Desert areas of Arizona and Mexico. The desert and mountain terrain of the museum is, of course, "natural" except where some animal habitats have had to be simulated in the museum's zoo.

There are views, and places to obtain views, all over this area. Not very far west of Tucson is the world-famous Kitt Peak Observatory, if you want *really* far out views. The Pinal Pioneer Parkway between Phoenix and Tucson passes through 30 miles of especially vivid Sonoran Desert landscape. Sabino Canyon in the Santa Catalina Mountains and Madera Canyon in the Santa Ritas are cool and beautiful places to

(Previous Full Page, Left:) The red and white sandstone cliffs of Oak Creek Canyon near Sedona form a theatrical backdrop for the canyon's vegetation.

(Previous Full Page, Right:) The Mittens stand out like thrones in Monument Valley, bathing in the golden light of the late afternoon sun.

view the rich bird life of the region. Madera, heavily forested with oak and sycamore, shelters hundreds of bird species. A trail from the canyon goes to the top of Mt. Wrightson, one of the area's higher eminences at 9,453 feet.

The heavy Indian and Spanish influence in the Tucson country is evident along the Santa Cruz River valley south from Tucson to the border. Here is Mission San Xavier del Bac, the twin-towered "White Dove of the Desert" founded in 1692. Farther south is Tubac, once a Spanish presidio, now an historical center and retirement town. South of Tubac is the restored ruin of Mission San Cayetano del Tumacacori, now a national monument.

Safford, 126 miles east of Tucson by road, is a convenient launch point for exploring some of the remote and rugged mountain and canyon country of southeastern Arizona. The primitive area of Aravaipa Valley over the Pinaleno Mountains from Safford is a great unspoiled area for the lover of the outdoors. The canyon is more than eight miles long and may be entered only by hikers, backpackers, and horseback riders. Hunters and cars are proscribed, insuring the quiet of the beautiful, cool haven.

The Pinaleno Mountains include Mt. Graham (10,717 feet), the highest point in southeast Arizona. A high forest road sweeps over the tops of these mountains, once again making possible one of those soul-refreshing long views of other mountains, desert and grassland.

Arizona's extreme southeast corner is full of names that are reminders of the state's colorful and sometimes violent history since the white man arrived. A number of roads that make up the Cochise Trail swing around Cochise Country in a 200-mile loop, touching at places that have given meaning to the word "colorful." The trail and the country are named for the great and legendary chief of the Chiricahua Apaches. One of the obvious stops on the route is Tombstone, a here-today, gone-tomorrow town that has become famous out of all proportion to its longevity. It lasted only about eight years, but as everyone knows, those were *some* eight years. The buildings are well-preserved, including the notorious OK Corral (the Earp brothers, Doc Holliday, *et al.* have moved elsewhere).

Not far from Tombstone is Bisbee, still a surface mining town after being the center of this mining area for nearly a century. Cochise Stronghold Recreation Area is north of Tombstone in Coronado National Forest. Here on high ground is a natural fortress where it was easy to keep track of the comings and goings of anyone or anything below.

Chiricahua National Monument, in the Chiricahua Mountains to the east, boasts especially scenic Bonita Canyon where erosion has created some weird and beautiful forms. A scenic drive takes in this and other visual feasts spread through the monument. But wherever one goes on the Cochise Trail he is heading for a point of high interest, be it a marvelous view, an odd natural phenomenon, or a community that has lived a lot of history.

(Following Full Page:) Saguaro cactus stand like sentinels in Saguaro National Monument, with the evening sun soon to disappear behind the mountains.